500 LIFE QUOTES *from* FAMOUS WOMEN

For better living and inspiration

Table of Contents

Introduction 1

Inspiration / Motivation 3

Character / Integrity 11

Self-control, Meditation, Peace 14

Success 16

Strength 20

Humor / Laughter 30

Relationships 35

Art / Creativity 39

Courage 43

Individuality 54

Knowledge / Truth 59

Love, Hate, Gratitude 69

Power 72

Responsibility 76

Wisdom 78

Beauty 83

Time 85

Introduction

We all have a "passion".

One of mine is collecting, and sharing, quotes.

I hope you will enjoy this lovingly crafted collection.

A treasure trove of wisdom, offering a collection of powerful quotes from some of the most influential women in history. Thoughtfully divided into sections, providing readers with inspiration and guidance.

- **Inspiration / Motivation**: Ignite your passion and drive with words from women who have overcome great odds.
- **Character / Integrity**: Learn the importance of staying true to oneself through the insights of women known for their moral strength.
- **Self-control, Meditation, Peace**: Find tranquility and balance with quotes that encourage mindfulness and inner peace.
- **Success**: Discover the secrets to achieving your goals from women who have reached the pinnacle of their fields.
- **Strength**: Draw courage and resilience from those who have faced adversity with grace.
- **Humor / Laughter**: Enjoy a light-hearted look at life with quotes that bring a smile to your face.
- **Relationships**: Gain wisdom on love, friendship, and family from women who understand the complexities of human connections.
- **Art / Creativity**: Be inspired by the creative minds that have shaped our world with their artistic visions.
- **Courage**: Embrace bravery and boldness with quotes that encourage you to face your fears.
- **Individuality**: Celebrate your unique self with insights from women who have championed individuality.

- **Knowledge / Truth**: Seek truth and wisdom from those who have dedicated their lives to learning and teaching.
- **Love, Hate, Gratitude**: Navigate the spectrum of emotions with quotes that explore the depths of the human heart.
- **Power**: Understand the dynamics of power and how to wield it responsibly.
- **Responsibility**: Reflect on the importance of accountability and duty through the words of conscientious women.
- **Beauty**: Appreciate the diverse perspectives on beauty from women who see it in all its forms.
- **Time**: Contemplate the passage of time and how to make the most of it with timeless advice.
- **Wisdom**: Absorb the profound insights that only come with experience and reflection.

This book is a celebration of the female spirit, offering timeless advice and encouragement for every stage of life.

Whether you're seeking motivation, comfort, or a new perspective, 500 Life Quotes from Famous Women is your go-to guide for inspiration.

Inspiration / Motivation

Agatha Christie
I like living. I have sometimes been wildly, despairingly, acutely miserable, racked with sorrow; but through it all I still know quite certainly that just to be alive is a grand thing.

Decide … whether or not the goal is worth the risks involved. If it is, stop worrying.
Amelia Earhart

The most effective way to do it, is to do it. It's about taking those first steps in doing something. That's the most important step. Thinking about it won't help. The best way to reach our goals is to do something.
Amelia Earhart

The most difficult thing is the decision to act. The rest is merely tenacity.
Amelia Earhart

If you can dance and be free and not be embarrassed, you can rule the world.
Amy Poehler

If you don't see the book you want on the shelf, write it.
Beverly Cleary

Only I can change my life. No one can do it for me.
Carol Burnett

The way I see it, if you want the rainbow, you gotta put up with the rain!
Dolly Parton

I am glad that I paid so little attention to good advice; had I abided by it I might have been saved from some of my most valuable mistakes.
Edna St. Vincent Millay

No one can make you feel inferior without your consent.
Eleanor Roosevelt

None of us can know what we are capable of until we are tested.
Elizabeth Blackwell

If your dreams do not scare you, they are not big enough.
Ellen Johnson Sirleaf

What sets you apart can sometimes feel like a burden, and it's not. And a lot of the time, it's what makes you great.
Emma Stone

If you follow your heart, if you listen to your gut and if you extend your hand to help another — not for any agenda, but for the sake of humanity — you are going to find the truth.
Erin Brockovich

Frida Kahlo
*You deserve the best, the very best, because you are one
of the few people in this lousy world who are honest to
themselves, and that is the only thing that really counts.*

*When you get into a tight place and everything goes
against you, till it seems as though you could not hold on a
minute longer, never give up then, for that is just the place
and time that the tide will turn.*
Harriet Beecher Stowe

Every great dream begins with a dreamer.
Harriet Tubman

Life is either a daring adventure or nothing.
Helen Keller

*It's never too late—never too late to start over, never too
late to be happy.*
Jane Fonda

Jane Goodall
*What you do makes a difference, and you have to decide
what kind of difference you want to make.*

*Technique and ability alone do not get you to the top; it is
the willpower that is most important.*
Junko Tabei

*You never have to ask anyone permission to lead. When you
want to lead, you lead.*
Kamala Harris

*You're going to walk into many rooms where you may be
the only one who looks like you or who has had the
experiences you've had. So you use that voice and be
strong.*
Kamala Harris

*To love what you do and feel like it matters — how could
anything be more fun?*
Katharine Graham

*Risk! Risk anything! Care no more for the opinions of
others, for those voices. Do the hardest thing on earth for
you. Act for yourself. Face the truth.*
Katherine Mansfield

*Perhaps some detours aren't detours at all. Perhaps they
are actually the path.*
Katherine Wolf

*Whatever it is that you think you want to do, and whatever it
is that you think stands between you and that, stop making
excuses. You can do anything.*
Katia Beauchamp

You don't have to be positive all the time. It's perfectly okay to feel sad, angry, annoyed, frustrated, scared, or anxious. Having feelings doesn't make you a 'negative person'. It makes you human.
Lori Deschne

I choose to make the rest of my life the best of my life.
Louise Hay

I'd rather regret the things I've done than regret the things I haven't done.
Lucille Ball

I was taught to strive, not because there were any guarantees of success, but because the act of striving is in itself the only way to keep faith with life.
Madeleine Albright

Maya Angelou
My mission in life is not merely to survive, but to thrive; and to do so with some passion, some compassion, some humor, and some style.

Ask for what you want and be prepared to get it.
Maya Angelou

If you're always trying to be normal, you will never know how amazing you can be.
Maya Angelou

If you don't like something, change it. If you can't change it, change your attitude.
Maya Angelou

You never have to ask anyone permission to lead. When you want to lead, you lead.
Maya Angelou

The price of inaction is far greater than the cost of a mistake.
Meg Whitman

I alone cannot change the world, but I can cast a stone across the waters to create many ripples.
Mother Teresa

Women who believe in each other create armies that will win kingdoms and wars.
Nikita Gill

Above all, be the heroine of your life, not the victim.
Nora Ephron

The biggest adventure you can ever take is to live the life of your dreams.
Oprah Winfrey

*All you need to know is that the future is wide open and
you are about to create it by what you do.*
Pema Chödrön

*If you're one of those people who has that little voice in the
back of her mind saying, 'Maybe I could do [fill in the
blank],' don't tell it to be quiet. Give it a little room to grow,
and try to find an environment it can grow in.*
Reese Witherspoon

*Real change, enduring change, happens one step at a
time.*
Ruth Bader Ginsburg

*With a defeat, when you lose, you get up, you make it
better, you try again. That's what I do in life, when I get
down, when I get sick, I don't want to just stop. I keep
going and I try to do more. Everyone always says never
give up but you really have to take that to heart and really
do never definitely give up. Keep trying.*
Serena Williams

*I really think a champion is defined not by their wins but by
how they can recover when they fall.*
Serena Williams

*If they don't give you a seat at the table, bring a folding
chair.*
Shirley Chisholm

*You can waste your lives drawing lines. Or you can live your
life crossing them.*
Shonda Rhimes

You have to make your own luck. You make it in practice and with training and conditioning.
Simone Biles

Simone de Beauvoir
Change your life today. Don't gamble on the future, act now, without delay.

Character / Integrity

Anaïs Nin

My mission, should I choose to accept it, is to find peace with exactly who and what I am. To take pride in my thoughts, my appearance, my talents, my flaws and to stop this incessant worrying that I can't be loved as I am.

Responsibility to yourself means refusing to let others do your thinking, talking, and naming for you; it means learning to respect and use your own brains and instincts; hence, grappling with hard work.
Adrienne Rich

Frida Kahlo

Only one mountain can know the core of another mountain.

Georgia O'Keeffe

Where I was born and where and how I have lived is unimportant. It is what I have done with where I have been that should be of interest.

It's not enough to be nice in life. You've got to have nerve.
Georgia O'Keeffe

Be a first rate version of yourself, not a second rate version of someone else.
Judy Garland

Find something you're passionate about and keep tremendously interested in it.
Julia Child

Margaret Atwood
Men often ask me, 'Why are your female characters so paranoid?' It's not paranoia. It's recognition of their situation.

All these things set a standard of behavior that you don't necessarily wish to live up to. If you're put on a pedestal you're supposed to behave like a pedestal type of person. Pedestals actually have a limited circumference. Not much room to move around.
Margaret Atwood

When I'm hungry, I eat. When I'm thirsty, I drink. When I feel like saying something, I say it.
Madonna

Marie Curie

Be less curious about people and more curious about ideas.

I was taught that the way of progress was neither swift nor easy.
Marie Curie

Maya Angelou

All of us knows, not what is expedient, not what is going to make us popular, not what the policy is, or the company policy – but in truth each of us knows what is the right thing to do. And that's how I am guided.

Do the best you can until you know better. Then when you know better, do better.
Maya Angelou

❧   ☙

Whatever the problem, be part of the solution. Don't just sit around raising questions and pointing out obstacles.
Tina Fey

No need to hurry. No need to sparkle. No need to be anybody but oneself.
Virginia Woolf

Self-control, Meditation, Peace

Anaïs Nin

From the backstabbing co-worker to the meddling sister-in-law, you are in charge of how you react to the people and events in your life. You can either give negativity power over your life or you can choose happiness instead. Take control and choose to focus on what is important in your life. Those who cannot live fully often become destroyers of life.

I surround myself with silence. The silence is within me, it permeates my house, reaches beyond the surface of the outer walls and into the bordering woods. It is one silence, continuous from within me outward in all directions… In the silence I listen, I watch, I sense, I attend, I observe. I require this silence. I search it out.
Alice Koller

The soul always knows what to do to heal itself. The challenge is to silence the mind.
Caroline Myss

Georgia O'Keeffe

The morning is the best time, there are no people around. My pleasant disposition likes the world with nobody in it.

*There is a silence into which the world cannot intrude.
There is an ancient peace you carry in your heart and have
not lost.*
Helen Schucman

*Like water which can clearly mirror the sky and the trees
only so long as its surface is undisturbed, the mind can
only reflect the true image of the Self when it is tranquil
and wholly relaxed.*
Indra Devi

*Have patience with everything that remains unsolved in
your heart. Try to love the questions themselves, like
locked rooms and like books written in a foreign language.
Do not now look for the answers. They cannot now be
given to you because you could not live with them.*
Rainer Maria Rilke

*Although the modes of meditation may appear to be
different from one another, in the end all of them become
one. There is no need to doubt this. One may adopt that
path which suits the maturity of one's mind.*
Ramana Maharshi

Success

One of the most important things I have learned is that businesses don't fail, entrepreneurs give up. Now sometimes, giving up is the right decision. But usually, you just need to dig in and figure out how to make things better. Remember: Every day is a new opportunity to get up and do it better than yesterday!
Adda Birnir

People respond well to those that are sure of what they want.
Anna Wintour

Define success on your own terms, achieve it by your own rules and build a life you're proud to live.
Anne Sweeney

The difference between successful people and others is how long they spend time feeling sorry for themselves.
Barbara Corcoran

Champions keep playing until they get it right.
Billie Jean King

The most successful entrepreneurs I know are optimistic. It's part of the job description.
Caterina Fake

*No one ever became a success without taking chances…
One must be able to recognize the moment and seize it
without delay.*
Estée Lauder

*I attribute my success to this: I never gave or took any
excuse.*
Florence Nightingale

*Don't just stand for the success of other women – insist
on it.*
Gail Blanke

*Make the most of yourself by fanning the tiny, inner sparks
of possibility into flames of achievement.*
Golda Meir

*There are two kinds of people: those who do the work and
those who take the credit. Try to be in the first group;
there is less competition there.*
Indira Gandhi

*Success doesn't come from what you do occasionally. It
comes from what you do consistently.*
Marie Forleo

*Don't cut off your career branches too early. Don't step
away from your career based on what 'might' happen.*
Mary Barra

I learned a long time ago that there is something worse than missing the goal, and that's not pulling the trigger.
Mia Hamm

Define goal. Take action. Stay focused. Expect success. Nothing less.
Michele Ruiz

People don't take opportunities because the timing is bad, the financial side unsecure. Too many people are overanalyzing. Sometimes you just have to go for it.
Michelle Zatlyn

Do not wait for leaders; do it alone, person to person. Be faithful in small things, because it is in them that your strength lies.
Mother Teresa

You create opportunities by performing, not complaining.
Muriel Siebert

To stay ahead, you must have your next idea waiting in the wings.
Rosabeth Moss Kanter

If you're not making some notable mistakes along the way, you're certainly not taking enough business and career chances.
Sallie Krawcheck

Do the best you can in every task, no matter how unimportant it may seem at the time. No one learns more about a problem than the person at the bottom.
Sandra Day O'Connor

Careers are a jungle gym, not a ladder.
Sheryl Sandberg

Simone de Beauvoir
If you live long enough, you'll see that every victory turns into a defeat.

Success isn't about the end result, it's about what you learn along the way.
Vera Wang

Strength

My words will either attract a strong mind or offend a weak one.
Anne Sexton

Feminism is for everybody.
Bell Hooks

Who knows what women can be when they are finally free to be themselves.
Betty Friedan

Whatever women do they must do twice as well as men to be thought of half as good. Luckily, this is not difficult.
Charlotte Whitton

Women have to harness their power – it's absolutely true. It's just learning not to take the first 'no'. And if you can't go straight ahead, you go around the corner.
Cher

I have chosen to no longer be apologetic for my femaleness and my femininity. And I want to be respected in all of my femaleness because I deserve to be.
Chimamanda Ngozi Adichie

Women have always been the strong ones of the world.
Coco Chanel

Women, if the soul of the nation is to be saved, I believe you must become its soul.
Coretta Scott King

If your actions create a legacy that inspires others to dream more, learn more, do more and become more, then, you are an excellent leader.
Dolly Parton

I'm not going to limit myself just because people won't accept the fact that I can do something else.
Dolly Parton

Friends. Sisters. Mothers. Professors. When women affirm women, it unlocks our power.
Elaine Welteroth

A woman is like a tea bag – you can't tell how strong she is until you put her in hot water.
Eleanor Roosevelt

Frida Kahlo
At the end of the day, we can endure much more than we think we can.

Dear Superwoman, let no one demean your intelligence. Let no one dribble you from your happiness. Let no one derail you from success. Be a smart, courageous, and determined woman.
Gift Gugu Mona

You are not supposed to be happy all the time. Life hurts and it's hard. Not because you're doing it wrong, but because it hurts for everybody. Don't avoid the pain. You need it.
Glennon Doyle

I have yet to hear a man ask for advice on how to combine marriage and a career.
Gloria Steinem

If women are supposed to be less rational and more emotional at the beginning of our menstrual cycle when the female hormone is at its lowest level, then why isn't it logical to say that, in those few days, women behave the most like the way men behave all month long?
Gloria Steinem

Men need marriage more than women do. In fact, they need it to survive.
Hanna Rosin

Women have discovered that they cannot rely on men's chivalry to give them justice.
Helen Keller

*To all the little girls who are watching this, never doubt that
you are valuable and powerful, and deserving of every
chance and opportunity in the world to pursue and achieve
your own dreams.*
Hillary Clinton

*We need to understand that there is no formula for how
women should lead their lives. That is why we must
respect the choices that each woman makes for herself
and her family.*
Hillary Clinton

*Her own thoughts and reflections were habitually her best
companions.*
Jane Austen

*I am a woman and a warrior. If you think I can't be both,
you've been lied to.*
Jennifer Zeynab Joukhadar

Behind every great woman ... is another great woman.
Kate Hodges

Well-behaved women seldom make history.
Laurel Thatcher Ulrich

*You deserve to be here. You deserve to exist. You deserve
to take up space in this world of men.*
MacKenzi Lee

*It took me quite a long time to develop a voice, and now
that I have it, I am not going to be silent.*
Madeleine Albright

*I raise up my voice—not so that I can shout, but so that
those without a voice can be heard…We cannot all succeed
when half of us are held back.*
Malala Yousafzai

*We realize the importance of our voices only when we are
silenced.*
Malala Yousafzai

৬৩   ৫৩

*Nothing I accept about myself can be used against me to
diminish me. When a woman rises up in glory, her energy is
magnetic and her sense of possibility contagious.*
Marianne Williamson

Marie Curie
*Life is not easy for any of us. But what of that? We must
have perseverance and above all confidence in ourselves.
We must believe that we are gifted for something and that
this thing must be attained   .*

*One of the best things that ever happened to me is that I'm
a woman. That is the way all females should feel.*
Marilyn Monroe

*If you can't handle me at my worst, then you sure as hell
don't deserve me at my best.*
Marilyn Monroe

*I always did something I was a little not ready to do. I think
that's how you grow. When there's that moment of 'Wow, I'm
not really sure I can do this,' and you push through those
moments, that's when you have a breakthrough.*
Marissa Mayer

*Strengthen the female mind by enlarging it, and there will be
an end to blind obedience.*
Mary Wollstonecraft

*Women are repeatedly accused of taking things personally. I
cannot see any other honest way of taking them.*
Marya Mannes

*We know that when a woman speaks truth to power, there
will be attempts to put her down… I'm not going to go
anywhere.*
Maxine Waters

Maya Angelou
*Each time a woman stands up for herself, without knowing it
possibly, without claiming it, she stands up for all women.*

Women don't need to find a voice, they have a voice, and they need to feel empowered to use it, and people need to be encouraged to listen.
Meghan Markle

A woman with a voice is, by definition, a strong woman.
Melinda Gates

There is no limit to what we, as women, can accomplish.
Michelle Obama

I hope you will find some way to break the rules and make a little trouble out there. And I also hope that you will choose to make some of that trouble on behalf of women.
Nora Ephron

I want all the girls without an exception to have that space for themselves where they have opportunities to be the women they wish to be.
Priyanka Chopra

After centuries of dormancy, young women can now look toward a future moulded by their own hands.
Rita Levi-Montalcini

My mother told me to be a lady. And for her, that meant be your own person, be independent.
Ruth Bader Ginsberg

If any female feels she need anything beyond herself to legitimate and validate her existence, she is already giving away her power to be selfdefining, her agency.
Ruth Bader Ginsburg

I long to speak out about the intense inspiration that comes to me from the lives of strong women. They have made of their lives an intense adventure.
Ruth Benedict

There are lots of opportunities out there for women to work in these fields; girls just need support, encouragement and mentoring to follow through with the sciences.
Sally Ride

As women achieve power, the barriers will fall. As society sees what women can do, as women see what women can do, there will be more women out there doing things, and we'll all be better off for it.
Sandra Day O'Connor

When you help a woman fulfil her potential, magic happens.
Sara Blakely

Don't be intimidated by what you don't know. That can be your greatest strength and ensure that you do things differently from everyone else.
Sara Blakely

You should never be surprised when someone treats you with respect. You should expect it.
Sarah Dessen

Every woman's success should be an inspiration to another. We're strongest when we cheer each other on. Don't just stand for the success of other women – insist on it.
Serena Williams

We need women at all levels, including the top, to change the dynamic, reshape the conversation, to make sure women's voices are heard and heeded, not overlooked and ignored.
Sheryl Sandberg

Tremendous amounts of talent are being lost to our society just because that talent wears a skirt.
Shirley Chisholm

I have as much muscle as any man, and can do as much work as any man.
Sojourner Truth

I think the girl who is able to earn her own living and pay her own way should be as happy as anybody on Earth. The sense of independence and security is very sweet.
Susan B. Anthony

As it turns out, social scientists have established only one fact about single women's mental health: employment improves it.
Susan Faludi

Women have the right to say: this is surface, this falsifies reality, this degrades.
Tillie Olsen

I don't think a female running a house is a problem, a broken family. It's perceived as one because of the notion that a head is a man.
Toni Morrison

We are volcanoes. When we women offer our experience as our truth, as human truth, all the maps change. There are new mountains.
Ursula K. Le Guin

Do not live someone else's life and someone else's idea of what womanhood is. Womanhood is you.
Viola Davis

Humor / Laughter

Agatha Christie
*I know there's a proverb which that says 'To err is human,'
but a human error is nothing to what a computer can do if it
tries.*

*No woman gets an orgasm from shining the kitchen floor.
Betty Freidan*

*My mother always used to say, 'The older you get, the
better you get. Unless you're a banana.'
Betty White*

*While gossip among women is universally ridiculed as low
and trivial, gossip among men, especially if it is about
women, is called theory, or idea, or fact.
Andrea Dworkin*

*We laugh and laugh, and nothing can ever be sad, no one
can be lost, or dead, or far away: right now we are here,
and nothing can mar our perfection, or steal the joy of this
perfect moment.
Audrey Niffenegger*

*I only began to sing because I couldn't get a job as an
actress.
Barbra Streisand*

A person who can bring the spirit of laughter into a room is indeed blessed.
Bennett Cerf

I'm not offended by all the dumb blonde jokes because I know I'm not dumb...and I also know that I'm not blonde.
Dolly Parton

Some minds remain open long enough for the truth not only to enter but to pass on through by way of a ready exit without pausing anywhere along the route.
Elizabeth Kenny

Laugh, and the world laughs with you;
Weep, and you weep alone;
For the sad old earth must borrow its mirth,
But has trouble enough of its own.
Ella Wheeler Wilcox

If you can laugh at it, you can live with it.
Erma Bombeck

If you can't make it better, you can laugh at it.
Erma Bombeck

Frida Kahlo
Nothing is worth more than laughter. It is strength to laugh and to abandon oneself, to be light.

She knew what all smart women knew: Laughter made you live better and longer.
Gail Parent

The truth will set you free. But first, it will piss you off.
Gloria Steinem

Once you can laugh at your own weaknesses, you can move forward. Comedy breaks down walls. It opens up people. If you're good, you can fill up those openings with something positive. Maybe you can combat some of the ugliness in the world.
Goldie Hawn

That is the best - to laugh with someone because you both think the same things are funny.
Gloria Vanderbilt

A woman without a man is like a fish without a bicycle.
Irina Dunn

Jane Goodall
It actually doesn't take much to be considered a difficult woman. That's why there are so many of us.

Humor and laughter are not necessarily the same thing. Humor permits us to see into life from a fresh and gracious perspective. We learn to take ourselves more lightly in the presence of good humor. Humor gives us the strength to bear what cannot be changed, and the sight to see the human under the pompous.
Joan Chittister

Life can be wildly tragic at times, and I've had my share. But whatever happens to you, you have to keep a slightly comic attitude. In the final analysis, you have got not to forget to laugh.
Katharine Hepburn

If truth is beauty, how come no one has their hair done in the library?
Lily Tomlin

I have always felt that laughter in the face of reality is probably the finest sound there is and will last until the day when the game is called on account of darkness. In this world, a good time to laugh is any time you can.
Linda Ellerbee

Good sex is like good Bridge. If you don't have a good partner, you'd better have a good hand.
Mae West

I'm single because I was born that way.
Mae West

If you want something said, ask a man. If you want something done, ask a woman.
Margaret Thatcher

Marie Curie

There are sadistic scientists who hurry to hunt down errors instead of establishing the truth.

The truth is, I've never fooled anyone. I've let men sometimes fool themselves.
Marilyn Monroe

He who laughs, lasts.
Mary Pettibone Poole

Behind every great man, there is a surprised woman.
Maryon Pearson

Maya Angelou

Laugh as much as possible, always laugh. It's the sweetest thing one can do for oneself & one's fellow human beings.

The desire to get married is a basic and primal instinct in women. It's followed by another basic and primal instinct: the desire to be single again.
Nora Ephron

The beauty of the world, which is so soon to perish, has two edges, one of laughter, one of anguish, cutting the heart asunder.
Virginia Woolf

Relationships

Agatha Christie

It is a curious thought, but it is only when you see people looking ridiculous that you realize just how much you love them.

I have learned not to worry about love; but to honor its coming with all my heart.
Alice Walker

Don't wait around for other people to be happy for you. Any Happiness you get you've got to make yourself.
Alice Walker

Once we recognize what it is we are feeling, once we recognize we can feel deeply, love deeply, can feel joy, then we will demand that all parts of our lives produce that kind of joy.
Audre Lorde

The love expressed between women is particular and powerful because we have had to love in order to live; love has been our survival.
Audre Lorde

Love is an endless act of forgiveness. Forgiveness is me giving up the right to hurt you for hurting me.
Beyoncé

The giving of love is an education in itself.
Eleanor Roosevelt

To be fully seen by somebody, then, and be loved anyhow —
this is a human offering that can border on miraculous.
Elizabeth Gilbert

I do not like the man who squanders life for fame; give me
the man who living makes a name.
Emily Dickinson

Frida Kahlo

Nothing is worth more than laughter. It is strength to laugh
and to abandon oneself, to be light. Tragedy is the most
ridiculous thing.

Perhaps we are in this world to search for love, find it and
lose it, again and again. With each love, we are born anew,
and with each love that ends, we collect a new wound. I am
covered with proud scars.
Isabel Allende

You don't love someone because they're perfect, you love
them in spite of the fact that they're not.
Jodi Picoult

We can improve our relationships with others by leaps and
bounds if we become encouragers instead of critics.
Joyce Meyer

Sometimes I wonder if men and women really suit each other. Perhaps they should live next door and just visit now and then.
Katharine Hepburn

Too many girls rush into relationships because of the fear of being single, then start making compromises, and losing their identity. Don't do that.
Katy Perry

Be honest, brutally honest. That is what's going to maintain relationships.
Lauryn Hill

Learn to be quiet enough to hear the genuine in yourself, so that you can hear it in others.
Marian Wright Edelman

Maya Angelou
I've learned that people will forget what you said, people will forget what you did, but people will never forget how you made them feel.

Do not bring people in your life who weigh you down, and trust your instincts. Good relationships feel good. They feel right. They don't hurt. They're not painful. That's not just with somebody you want to marry, but it's with the friends you choose. It's with the people you surround yourself with.
Michelle Obama

The greatest thing you'll ever learn is to love and be loved in return.
Natalie Cole

Surround yourself with only people who are going to lift you higher.
Oprah Winfrey

You've got to learn to leave the table when love's no longer being served.
Nina Simone

The cowards and the impatient can enjoy one night stands as it takes a great deal of patience, unconditional love, trust, fearlessness and a deep sense of individuality to maintain relationships.
Sherlyn Chopra

I don't need anyone to rectify my existence. The most profound relationship we will ever have is the one with ourselves.
Shirley MacLaine

Fall in love with someone who makes you glad to be different.
Sue Zhao

Art / Creativity

Agatha Christie
*I don't think necessity is the mother of invention. Invention . . .
arises directly from idleness, possibly also from laziness. To
save oneself trouble.*

Take any challenge as a creative opportunity.
Alexandra Watkins

*Turn your demons into art, your shadow into a friend, your
failures into teachers, your weaknesses into reasons to keep
fighting. Don't waste your pain. Recycle your heart.*
Andrea Balt

*I've learned that time is my most valuable resource. How I
spend it, where I spend it, and who I spend it with is the key to
making me feel whole as a leader, parent, creative partner, and
friend.*
Andrea Jacobs

*Art is something that makes you breathe with a different kind
of happiness.*
Anni Albers

*There is no recipe, there is no one way to do things — there is
only your way. And if you can recognize that in yourself and
accept and appreciate that in others, you can make magic.*
Ara Katz

The audience is the best judge of anything. They cannot be lied to. Truth brings them closer. A moment that lags – they're gonna cough.
Barbra Streisand

Like the sand and the oyster, it's a creative irritant. In each poem, I'm trying to reveal a truth, so it can't have a fictional beginning.
Carol Ann Duffy

Everyone has creativity within them. It's just a matter of unlocking that creativity
Christina Canters

Creativity is an ongoing process. When I first started in my role, I found a quote in a magazine that resonated with me. It said "Use your imagination." I cut it out and taped it on my computer monitor. Sixteen years have passed and I am still reminded daily that the success of our company is founded on being open and receptive to creativity and the inevitability of change.
Cyndie Martini

I don't know much about creative writing programs. But they're not telling the truth if they don't teach, one, that writing is hard work, and, two, that you have to give up a great deal of life, your personal life, to be a writer.
Doris Lessing

People hate their own art because it looks like they made it. They think if they get better, it will stop looking like they made it. A better person made it. But there's no level of skill beyond which you stop being you. You hate the most valuable thing about your art.
Elicia Donze

Technology is simply a tool supporting human brilliance.
Gail S. Ayers

Georgia O'Keeffe
I found I could say things with color and shapes that I couldn't say any other way... things I had no words for.

Poetry is a political act because it involves telling the truth.
June Jordan

Creativity and invention are the mother's milk of success for the future.
Lisa Picard

Margaret Atwood
What matters is how the art makes you feel.

Any novel is hopeful in that it presupposes a reader. It is, actually, a hopeful act just to write anything, really, because you're assuming that someone will be around to [read] it.
Margaret Atwood

The genesis of a poem for me is usually a cluster of words. The only good metaphor I can think of is a scientific one: dipping a thread into a supersaturated solution to induce crystal formation.
Margaret Atwood

Maya Angelou
You can't use up creativity. The more you use it, the more you have.

Creativity is born of the desperate, immutable, hopeless and untenable need to understand humanity, the world, and its machinations.
Naomi Ladizinsky

The secret to life is to put your self in the right lighting. For some, it's a Broadway spotlight; for others, a lamplit desk. Use your natural powers - of persistence, concentration, and insight - to do work you love and work that matters. Solve problems. Make art. Think deeply.
Susan Cain

Some people will always be deaf to your song. Don't stop signing.
Trudy Jane

The creative adult is the child who survived.
Ursula K. Le Guin

I talk about the gods, I am an atheist. But I am an artist too, and therefore a liar. Distrust everything I say. I am telling the truth.
Ursula K. Le Guin

Courage

Agatha Christie

You cannot give to people what they are incapable of receiving.

They'll tell you you're too loud – that you need to wait your turn and ask the right people for permission. Do it anyway.
Alexandria Ocasio Cortez

Anais Nin

Life shrinks or expands in proportion to one's courage.

We are always forcing others to be what we want, need, imagine, and we never forgive them for being themselves.
Anaïs Nin

Courage is the price that life exacts for granting peace.
Amelia Earhart

You could certainly say that I've never underestimated myself. There's nothing wrong with being ambitious.
Angela Merkel

*Dead people receive more flowers than the living ones
because regret is stronger than gratitude.*
Anne Frank

*Fearlessness is like a muscle. I know from my own life that
the more I exercise it the more natural it becomes to not let
my fears run me.*
Arianna Huffington

*You should never let your fears prevent you from doing what
you know is right.*
Aung San Suu Kyi

*The question isn't who's going to let me; it's who is going to
stop me.*
Ayn Rand

*Dominator culture has tried to keep us all afraid, to make us
choose safety instead of risk, sameness instead of diversity.
Moving through that fear, finding out what connects us,
revelling in our differences; this is the process that brings us
closer, that gives us a world of shared values, of meaningful
community.*
Bell Hooks

*Courage, sacrifice, determination, commitment, toughness,
heart, talent, guts. That's what little girls are made of; the
heck with sugar and spice.*
Bethany Hamilton

*Vulnerability is the birthplace of love, belonging, joy,
courage, empathy, and creativity.*
Brené Brown

The truth is: Belonging starts with self-acceptance. Your level of belonging, in fact, can never be greater than your level of self-acceptance, because believing that you're enough is what gives you the courage to be authentic, vulnerable and imperfect.
Brené Brown

Do not be afraid to make decisions. Do not be afraid to make mistakes.
Carly Fiorina

One of the most calming and powerful actions you can do to intervene in a stormy world is to stand up and show your soul.
Clarissa Pinkola Estés

The most courageous act is still to think for yourself. Aloud.
Coco Chanel

You gain strength, courage and confidence by every experience in which you really stop to look fear in the face. You are able to say to yourself, 'I have lived through this horror. I can take the next thing that comes along.' You must do the thing you think you cannot do.
Eleanor Roosevelt

You're afraid of surrender because you don't want to lose control. But you never had control. All you had was anxiety.
Elizabeth Gilbert

"Finding yourself" is not really how it works. You aren't a ten-dollar bill in last winter's coat pocket. You are also not lost. Your true self is right there, buried under cultural conditioning, other people's opinions, and inaccurate conclusions you drew as a kid that became your beliefs about who you are. "Finding yourself" is actually returning to yourself. An unlearning, an excavation, a remembering who you were before the world got its hands on you.
Emily McDowell

If you don't risk anything, you risk even more.
Erica Jong

Frida Kahlo
At the end of the day, we can endure much more than we think we can.

Pain, pleasure and death are no more than a process for existence. The revolutionary struggle in this process is a doorway open to intelligence.
Frida Kahlo

Energy moves in waves. Waves move in patterns. Patterns move in rhythms. A human being is just that energy, waves, patterns, rhythms. Nothing more. Nothing less. A dance.
Gabrielle Roth

Georgia O'Keeffe
To create one's own world takes courage.

*I have already settled it for myself so flattery and criticism
go down the same drain and I am quite free.*
Georgia O'Keefe

*I've been absolutely terrified every moment of my life and
I've never let it keep me from doing a single thing that I
wanted to do.*
Georgia O'Keeffe

*I wish people were all trees and I think I could enjoy them
then.*
Georgia O'Keeffe

*I think it's so foolish for people to want to be happy.
Happy is so momentary--you're happy for an instant and
then you start thinking again. Interest is the most
important thing in life; happiness is temporary, but interest
is continuous.*
Georgia O'Keefe

*Be messy and complicated and afraid and show up
anyways.*
Glennon Doyle

*The trouble with lying and deceiving is that their efficiency
depends entirely upon a clear notion of the truth that the
liar and deceiver wishes to hide.*
Hannah Arendt

*Avoiding danger is no safer in the long run than outright
exposure. The fearful are caught as often as the bold.*
Helen Keller

There is a stubbornness about me that can never bear to be frightened at the will of others. My courage always rises at every attempt to intimidate me.
Jane Austen

Jane Goodall
You cannot get through a single day without having an impact on the world around you. What you do makes a difference, and you have to decide what kind of difference you want to make.

What makes us human, I think, is an ability to ask questions, a consequence of our sophisticated spoken language.
Jane Goodall

Homo sapiens is the species that invents symbols in which to invest passion and authority, then forgets that symbols are inventions.
Joyce Carol Oates

By having the courage to take the first step into rooms, circles, and conversations where you may feel like you don't belong, you also open the door for others to contribute their diverse perspectives, creating more meaningful, collaborative solutions for today and beyond.
Kim Vu

Our fear of the unknown and our fear of making mistakes trick us into focusing on what we don't know or can't do. When we give ourselves the freedom to be uncertain and less than perfect, then we can start thinking, "What do I know? What can I do?" That's when the adventure starts — learning, thriving, conquering, failing, recouping, and having a ton of fun.
Kristin Smith

Margaret Atwood
Optimism means better than reality; pessimism means worse than reality. I'm a realist.

...each person has a 'story'—a personal narrative—which is constantly being replayed, revised, taken apart and put together again. The significant points in this narrative change as a person ages—what may have been tragedy at 20 is seen as comedy or nostalgia at 40.
Margaret Atwood

But remember that forgiveness too is a power. To beg for it is a power, and to withhold or bestow it is a power, perhaps the greatest.
Margaret Atwood

Marie Curie
Nothing in life is to be feared, it is only to be understood. Now is the time to understand more, so that we may fear less.

*More than whimsy, joy is a weapon we use to fight life's
battles.*
Margaret Feinberg

*Courage doesn't always roar. Sometimes courage is the little
voice at the end of the day that says I'll try again tomorrow.*
Mary Anne Radmacher

*There are two things people want more than sex and
money…recognition and praise.*
Mary Kay Ash

*There is but one solution to the intricate riddle of life; to
improve ourselves, and contribute to the happiness of others.*
Mary Shelley

Maya Angelou
*You may not control all the events that happen to you, but
you can decide not to be reduced by them.*

*I've learned that making a 'living' is not the same thing as
'making a life'.*
Maya Angelou

We need much less than we think we need.
Maya Angelou

*It's one of the greatest gifts you can give yourself, to forgive.
Forgive everybody.*
Maya Angelou

Think like a queen. A queen is not afraid to fail. Failure is another stepping stone to greatness.
Oprah Winfrey

I have enough for this life. If there is no other life, then this one has been enough to make worth being born, myself a human being.
Pearl S. Buck

I have learned over the years that when one's mind is made up, this diminishes fear; knowing what must be done does away with fear.
Rosa Parks

You must never be fearful about what you are doing when it's right.
Rosa Parks

ॐ   ॐ

Courage is like a muscle. We strengthen it by use.
Ruth Gordon

So please ask yourself: What would I do if I weren't afraid? And then go do it.
Sheryl Sandberg

Cautious, careful people, always casting about to preserve their reputations, can never effect a reform.
Susan B. Anthony

Those who do not move, do not notice their chains.
Rosa Luxemburg

Simone de Beauvoir

Representation of the world, like the world itself, is the work of men; they describe it from their own point of view, which they confuse with the absolute truth.

One is not born, but rather becomes, a woman.
Simone de Beauvoir

Society cares about the individual only in so far as he is profitable. The young know this. Their anxiety as they enter in upon social life matches the anguish of the old as they are excluded from it.
Simone de Beauvoir

I took a deep breath and listened to the old brag of my heart. I am, I am, I am.
Sylvia Plath

Imagine you are walking in the woods and you see a small dog sitting by a tree. As you approach it, it suddenly lunges at you, teeth bared. You are frightened and angry. But then you notice that one of its legs is caught in a trap. Immediately your mood shifts from anger to concern. You see that the dog's aggression is coming from a place of vulnerability and pain. This applies to all of us. When we behave in hurtful ways, it is because we are caught in some kind of trap. The more we look through the eyes of wisdom at ourselves and one another, the more we cultivate a compassionate heart.
Tara Brach

*To me, "Fearless" is not the absence of fear. It's not being completely unafraid. To me, fearless is having fears.
Fearless is having doubts. Lots of them.
Taylor Swift*

*There is no gate, no lock, no bolt that you can set upon the freedom of my mind.
Virginia Woolf*

Individuality

Autism doesn't have to define a person. Artists with autism are like anyone else: They define themselves through hard work and individuality.
Adrienne Bailon

Agatha Christie

Very few of us are what we seem.

Our uniqueness makes us special, makes perception valuable – but it can also make us lonely. This loneliness is different from being 'alone': You can be lonely even surrounded by people. The feeling I'm talking about stems from the sense that we can never fully share the truth of who we are. I experienced this acutely at an early age.
Amy Tan

Anais Nin

Truth is something which can't be told in a few words. Those who simplify the universe only reduce the expansion of its meaning.

There are very few human beings who receive the truth, complete and staggering, by instant illumination. Most of them acquire it fragment by fragment, on a small scale, by successive developments, cellularly, like a laborious mosaic.
Anais Nin

Accuracy of language is one of the bulwarks of truth.
Anna Jameson

What is done cannot be undone, but one can prevent it happening again.
Anne Frank

Your problem is how you are going to spend this one odd and precious life you have been issued. Whether you're going to spend it trying to look good and creating the illusion that you have power over people and circumstances, or whether you are going to taste it, enjoy it and find out the truth about who you are.
Anne Lamott

You don't have to sort of enhance reality. There is nothing stranger than truth.
Annie Leibovitz

The truth is not for all men, but only for those who seek it.
Ayn Rand

I don't care what you think about me. I don't think about you at all.
Coco Chanel

What is genius but the power of expressing a new individuality? Elizabeth
Barrett Browning

As soon as something becomes 'trendy,' I go off it. I hate the idea of being a sheep and just following a look because I've been told it's fashionable. Individuality makes the world a much more interesting place.
Eliza Doolittle

*American poetry, like American painting, is always personal
with an emphasis on the individuality of the poet.*
Diane Wakoski

*The higher mental development of woman, the less possible it
is for her to meet a congenial male who will see in her, not
only sex, but also the human being, the friend, the comrade
and strong individuality, who cannot and ought not lose a
single trait of her character.*
Emma Goldman

Georgia O'Keefe

I decided to accept as true my own thinking.

*I have things in my head that are not like what anyone taught
me — shapes and ideas so near to me, so natural to my way
of being and thinking.*
Georgia O'Keefe

*I can't live where I want to, I can't go where I want to go, I
can't do what I want to, I can't even say what I want to. I
decided I was a very stupid fool not to at least paint as I
wanted to.*
Georgia O'Keefe

*Someone else's vision will never be as good as your own
vision of yourself. Live and die with it 'cause in the end it's all
you have. Lose it and you lose yourself and everything else. I
should have listened to myself.*
Georgia O'Keefe

I know now that most people are so closely concerned with themselves that they are not aware of their own individuality, I can see myself, and it has helped me to say what I want to say in paint.
Georgia O'Keeffe

I believe in individuality, that everybody is special, and it's up to them to find that quality and let it live.
Grace Jones

Men have been found to resist the most powerful monarchs and to refuse to bow down before them, but few indeed have been found to resist the crowd, to stand up alone before misguided masses, to face their implacable frenzy without weapons and with folded arms to dare a no when a yes is demanded. Such a man was Zola!
Hannah Arendt

Love, with very young people, is a heartless business. We drink at that age from thirst, or to get drunk; it is only later in life that we occupy ourselves with the individuality of our wine.
Karen Blixen

To be yourself is truly a revolutionary act, and I think more and more people should try it, because it's gotten me a pretty cool life.
Lena Waithe

Our uniqueness, our individuality, and our life experience molds us into fascinating beings. I hope we can embrace that. I pray we may all challenge ourselves to delve into the deepest resources of our hearts to cultivate an atmosphere of understanding, acceptance, tolerance, and compassion. We are all in this life together.
Linda Thompson

...what I have learned for myself is that I don't have to be anybody else; and that myself is good enough; and that when I am being true to that self, then I can avail myself to extraordinary things such as this, you know, that I didn't think was necessarily possible...and I think that's the thing. You have to allow for the impossible to be possible.
Lupita Nyong'o

I think the most powerful beauty is representative of uniqueness and individuality of every person.
Nikita Dragun

No need to hurry. No need to sparkle. No need to be anybody but oneself.
Virginia Woolf

You change the world by being yourself.
Yoko Ono

Knowledge / Truth

*When a woman tells the truth she is creating the possibility
for more truth around her.*
Adrienne Rich

*'False history gets made all day, any day, the truth of the
new is never on the news.*
Adrienne Rich

Agatha Christie
*Everything must be taken into account. If the fact will not fit
the theory - let the theory go. The truth, however ugly in
itself, is always curious and beautiful to seekers after it.*
Agatha Christie

*There's nothing so kingly as kindness, and nothing so royal
as truth.*
Alice Cary

*As long as the people don't fear the truth, there is hope. For
once they fear it, the one who tells it doesn't stand a
chance. And today, truth is still beautiful... but so
frightening.*
Alice Walker

*Pain reaches the heart with electrical speed, but truth
moves to the heart as slowly as a glacier.*
Barbara Kingsolver

The truth needs so little rehearsal.
Barbara Kingsolver

*Seeing is no longer believing. The very notion of truth has
been put into crisis. In a world bloated with images, we are
finally learning that photographs do indeed lie.*
Barbara Kruger

*There are new words now that excuse everybody. Give me
the good old days of heroes and villains, the people you
can bravo or hiss. There was a truth to them that all the
slick credulity of today cannot touch.*
Bette Davis

*Crazy-busy' is a great armor, it's a great way for numbing.
What a lot of us do is that we stay so busy, and so out in
front of our life, that the truth of how we're feeling and what
we really need can't catch up with us.*
Brené Brown

*A documentary film-maker can't help but use poetry to tell
the story. I bring truth to my fiction. These things go hand in
hand.*
Chloe Zhao

Hard times arouse an instinctive desire for authenticity.
Coco Chanel

To live in the light of a new day and an unimaginable and unpredictable future, you must become fully present to a deeper truth – not a truth from your head, but a truth from your heart; not a truth from your ego, but a truth from the highest source.
Debbie Ford

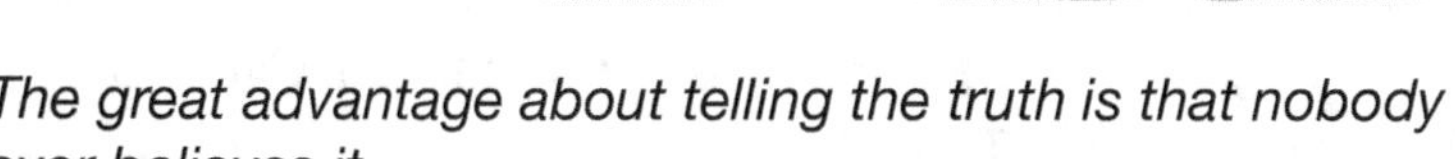

The great advantage about telling the truth is that nobody ever believes it.
Dorothy L. Sayers

My longing for truth was a single prayer.
Edith Stein

The aim of flattery is to soothe and encourage us by assuring us of the truth of an opinion we have already formed about ourselves.
Edith Sitwell

I've led a school whose faculty and students examine and discuss and debate every aspect of our law and legal system. And what I've learned most is that no one has a monopoly on truth or wisdom. I've learned that we make progress by listening to each other, across every apparent political or ideological divide.
Elena Kagan

The truth does not need to be defended.
Elisabeth Kubler-Ross

Nobody speaks the truth when there is something they must have.
Elizabeth Bowen

The moment we begin to fear the opinions of others and hesitate to tell the truth that is in us, and from motives of policy are silent when we should speak, the divine floods of light and life no longer flow into our souls.
Elizabeth Cady Stanton

Find out who you are and be that person. That's what your soul was put on this Earth to be. Find that truth, live that truth and everything else will come.
Ellen DeGeneres

Truth is so rare that it is delightful to tell it.
Emily Dickinson

When you learn that a truth is a lie, anger follows.
Grace Slick

The sad truth is that most evil is done by people who never make up their minds to be good or evil.
Hannah Arendt

After all, the ultimate goal of all research is not objectivity, but truth.
Helene Deutsch

There is no man more dangerous, in a position of power, than he who refuses to accept as a working truth the idea that all a man does should make for rightness and soundness, that even the fixing of a tariff rate must be moral.
Ida Tarbell

We live in a fantasy world, a world of illusion. The great task in life is to find reality.
Iris Murdoch

Seldom, very seldom, does complete truth belong to any human disclosure; seldom can it happen that something is not a little disguised, or a little mistaken.
Jane Austen

Jane Goodall
Words can be said in bitterness and anger, and often there seems to be an element of truth in the nastiness. And words don't go away, they just echo around.

I don't think that faith, whatever you're being faithful about, really can be scientifically explained. And I don't want to explain this whole life business through truth, science. There's so much mystery. There's so much awe.
Jane Goodall

Truth is always served by great minds, even if they fight it.
Jean Rostand

Children say that people are hung sometimes for speaking the truth.
Joan of Arc

It's so essential to happiness to speak your truth out loud – because this sharing of your core pain is what creates a necessary healing shift – from negative beliefs about the world – to positive beliefs – and frees you up to be able to fully view life with meaning, purpose and connection with others.
Karen Salmansohn

It's very easy to be judgmental until you know someone's truth.
Kate Winslet

I believe religion is a branch of spirituality, often misinterpreted and twisted to suit people's ideas. In truth, religion and spirituality are meant to co-exist happily.
Kay Kay Menon

We live in such a gullible world. Anything that's written, anything that's posted, anything picture that is interpreted one way is taken as truth.
Keri Hilson

Cynicism is an unpleasant way of saying the truth.
Lillian Hellman

We too often bind ourselves by authorities rather than by the truth.
Lucretia Mott

Now all we need is to continue to speak the truth fearlessly, and we shall add to our number those who will turn the scale to the side of equal and full justice in all things.
Lucy Stone

Because you're not what I would have you be, I blind myself to who, in truth, you are.
Madeleine L'Engle

Search for the truth is the noblest occupation of man; its publication is a duty.
Madame de Stael

Margaret Atwood

When I was young I believed that 'nonfiction' meant 'true.' But you read a history written in, say, 1920 and a history of the same events written in 1995 and they're very different. There may not be one Truth—there may be several truths—but saying that is not to say that reality doesn't exist.

Learning is always rebellion... Every bit of new truth discovered is revolutionary to what was believed before.
Margaret Lee Runbeck

Of course it's the same old story. Truth usually is the same old story.
Margaret Thatcher

My truth is that what doesn't kill you makes you weaker rather than stronger, although it makes you wiser.
Marian Keyes

Marie Curie

When radium was discovered, no one knew that it would prove useful in hospitals. The work was one of pure science. And this is a proof that scientific work must not be considered from the point of view of the direct usefulness of it.

Truth is strong, and sometime or other will prevail.
Mary Astell

The truth is, the harder you fight, the sweeter are the rewards in the end.
Mary Kom

I am not afraid of the pen, or the scaffold, or the sword. I will tell the truth wherever I please.
Mary Harris Jones

Clouds and darkness surround us, yet Heaven is just, and the day of triumph will surely come, when justice and truth will be vindicated.
Mary Todd Lincoln

Maya Angelou
There's a world of difference between truth and facts. Facts can obscure the truth.

We learned about honesty and integrity – that the truth matters… that you don't take shortcuts or play by your own set of rules… and success doesn't count unless you earn it fair and square.
Michelle Obama

The thing you fear most has no power. Your fear of it is what has the power. Facing the truth really will set you free.
Oprah Winfrey

You never find yourself until you face the truth.
Pearl Bailey

When I can look life in the eyes, grown calm and very coldly wise, life will have given me the truth, and taken in exchange – my youth.
Sara Teasdale

I pefer an ugly truth to a pretty lie. If someone is telling me the truth that is when I will give my heart.
Shakira

Simone de Beauvoir
I tore myself away from the safe comfort of certainties through my love for truth - and truth rewarded me.

Defending the truth is not something one does out of a sense of duty or to allay guilt complexes, but is a reward in itself.
Simone de Beauvoir

Representation of the world, like the world itself, is the work of men; they describe it from their own point of view, which they confuse with the absolute truth.
Simone de Beauvoir

Truth is often a multiplicity of perspectives, and sometimes the more viewpoints and versions of events there are, the closer the reader gets to an overarching truth.
Susan Barker

Truth is powerful and it prevails.
Sojourner Truth

*he word theatre comes from the Greeks. It means the
seeing place. It is the place people come to see the truth
about life and the social situation.*
Stella Adler

*What is truth? Truth doesn't really exist. Who is going to
judge whether my experience of an incident is more valid
than yours? No one can be trusted to be the judge of that.*
Tracey Emin

*If you do not tell the truth about yourself you cannot tell it
about other people.*
Virginia Woolf

*Mental fight means thinking against the current, not with it.
It is our business to puncture gas bags and discover the
seeds of truth.*
Virginia Woolf

*It is in our idleness, in our dreams, that the submerged
truth sometimes comes to the top.*
Virginia Woolf

*My mother taught me that when you stand in the truth and
someone tells a lie about you, don't fight it.*
Whitney Houston

*The stupid believe that to be truthful is easy; only the artist,
the great artist, knows how difficult it is.*
Willa Cather

Love, Hate, Gratitude

Agatha Christie

But surely for everything you love you have to pay some price.

A mother's love for her child is like nothing else in the world. It knows no law, no pity. It dares all things and crushes down remorselessly all that stands in its path.
Agatha Christie

ରୁ   ରୁ

I have learned not to worry about love; but to honor its coming with all my heart.
Alice Walker

Anaïs Nin

Age does not protect you from love. But love, to some extent, protects you from age.

I can only connect deeply or not at all.
Anaïs Nin

Your experiences will be yours alone. But truth and best friendship will rarely if ever disappoint you.
Anne Lamott

What separates privilege from entitlement is gratitude.
Brené Brown

Gratitude is a divine emotion: it fills the heart, but not to bursting; it warms it, but not to fever.
Charlotte Brontë

Love is like quicksilver in the hand. Leave the fingers open and it stays. Clutch it and it darts away.
Dorothy Parker

I think I fall in love a little bit with anyone who shows me their soul. This world is so guarded and fearful. I appreciate rawness so much.
Emery Allen

Georgia O'Keeffe
You are one of my nicest thoughts.

The truth is that there is only one terminal dignity – love. And the story of a love is not important – what is important is that one is capable of love. It is perhaps the only glimpse we are permitted of eternity.
Helen Hayes

For women the best aphrodisiacs are words. The G-spot is in the ears. He who looks for it below there is wasting his time.
Isabel Allende

For above all things Love means sweetness, and truth, and measure; yea, loyalty to the loved one and to your word. And because of this I dare not meddle with so high a matter.
Marie de France

Maya Angelou

Let gratitude be the pillow upon which you kneel to say your nightly prayer. And let faith be the bridge you build to overcome evil and welcome good

If you judge people, you have no time to love them.
Mother Teresa

Simone de Beauvoir

One's life has value so long as one attributes value to the life of others, by means of love, friendship, indignation and compassion.

Power

*It takes a long time to learn that a courtroom is the last place
in the world for learning the truth.*
Alice Koller

*The most common way people give up their power is by
thinking they don't have any.*
Alice Walker

*I am not free while any woman is unfree, even when her
shackles are very different from my own.*
Audre Lorde

*When I dare to be powerful, to use my strength in the
service of my vision, then it becomes less and less important
whether I am afraid.*
Audre Lorde

ରୁ   ଙ

*Sometimes people try to destroy you, precisely because
they recognize your power — not because they don't see it,
but because they see it and they don't want it to exist.*
Bell Hooks

Power's not given to you. You have to take it.
Beyoncé

*Politics, as a practice, whatever its profession, has always
been the systematic organization of hatreds.*
Brooks Adams

We must talk about poverty, because people insulated by their own comfort lose sight of it.
Dorothy Day

The ideal subject of totalitarian rule is not the convinced Nazi or the convinced Communist, but people for whom the distinction between fact and fiction (i.e., the reality of experience) and the distinction between true and false (i.e., the standards of thought) no longer exist.
Hannah Arendt

Everything is within your power, and your power is within you.
Janice Trachtman

Margaret Atwood
If I love you, is that a fact or a weapon?

Oppression involves a failure of the imagination: the failure to imagine the full humanity of other human beings.
Margaret Atwood

It is a dark, unspoken truth that the powerful – the 'ruling class' – make up the rules as they go along.
Marilyn Ferguson

No matter how difficult and painful it may be, nothing sounds as good to the soul as the truth.
Martha Beck

We know that when a woman speaks truth to power, there will be attempts to put her down… I'm not going to go anywhere.
Maxine Waters

Women belong in all places where decisions are being made. It shouldn't be that women are the exception. We need women at all levels, including the top, to change the dynamic, reshape the conversation, to make sure women's voices are heard and heeded, not overlooked and ignored.
Ruth Bader Ginsberg

Simone de Beauvoir
All oppression creates a state of war.

Man is defined as a human being and a woman as a female — whenever she behaves as a human being she is said to imitate the male.
Simone de Beauvoir

Brutal men with unlimited power are the same all over the world.
Mary Boykin Chesnut

I ask for no favor for my sex. All I ask of our brethren is that they take their feet off our necks.
Sarah Moore Grimké

The unreliable narrator is an odd concept. The way I see it, we're all unreliable narrators of our lives who usually have absolute trust in our self-told stories. Any truth is, after all, just a matter of perspective.
Sarah Pinborough

Words have power. TV has power. My pen has power.
Shonda Rhimes

Responsibility

Anaïs Nin

Had I not created my whole world, I would certainly have died in other people's.

Your problem is how you are going to spend this one and precious life you have been issued. Whether you're going to spend it trying to look good and creating the illusion that you have power over circumstances, or whether you are going to taste it, enjoy it and find out the truth about you are.
Anne Lamott

In the different voice of women lies the truth of an ethic of care, the tie between relationship and responsibility, and the origins of aggression in the failure of connection.
Carol Gilligan

Your wound is probably not your fault, but your healing is your responsibility.
Denice Frohman

Frida Kahlo

I think that little by little, I'll be able to solve my problems and survive.

Margaret Atwood

Nothing makes me more nervous than people who say, 'It can't happen here.' Anything can happen anywhere, given the right circumstances.

Marie Curie

You cannot hope to build a better world without improving the individuals. To that end, each of us must work for his own improvement and, at the same time, share a general responsibility for all humanity, our particular duty being to aid those to whom we think we can be most useful.

I live my life by one fundamental rule: You cannot change what other people do. You can only control your own behavior. Once you accept this, you accept ultimate responsibility for your own successes or failures — and this is the true characteristic of any leader.
Susan Ruszala

Simone de Beauvoir

Change your life today. Don't gamble on the future, act now, without delay.

Wisdom

Agatha Christie

The impossible could not have happened, therefore the impossible must be possible in spite of appearances.

The best teachers are those who show you where to look, but don't tell you what to see.
Alexandra K. Trenfor

In my life, I had come to realize that, when things were going very well, indeed, it was just the time to anticipate trouble. And, conversely, I learned from pleasant experience that at the most despairing crisis, when all looked sour beyond words, some delightful "break" was apt to lurk just around the corner.
Amelia Earhart

Anaïs Nin

What makes people despair is that they try to find a universal meaning to the whole of life, and then end up by saying it is absurd, illogical, and empty of meaning. There is not one big, cosmic meaning for all, there is only the meaning we each give to our life, an individual meaning, an individual plot, like an individual novel, a book for each person.

The dream was always running ahead of one. To catch up, to live for a moment in unison with it, that was the miracle.
Anaïs Nin

Brooke Medicine Eagle
Ancient teachings call us to turn primary attention to the Sacred Web of Life, of which we are part and with which we are so obviously entangled. This quality of attention - paying attention to the whole - is called among my people 'holiness'.

Take criticism seriously, but not personally. If there is truth or merit in the criticism, try to learn from it. Otherwise, let it roll right off you.
Hillary Clinton

Men and women are like right and left hands; it doesn't make sense not to use both.
Jeanette Rankin

You can't please everyone, and you can't make everyone like you.
Katie Couric

There's no such thing as perfection, and even if there were, I think it'd be rather boring.
Lorraine Heath

Conceit spoils the finest genius. There is not much danger that real talent or goodness will be overlooked long; even if it is, the consciousness of possessing and using it well should satisfy one, and the great charm of all power is modesty.
Louisa May Alcott

Maya Angelou
Everything in the universe has rhythm. Everything dances.

Every storm runs out of rain.
Maya Angelou

Life is a game play it... Life is too precious, do not destroy it.
Mother Teresa

Simone de Beauvoir
One is not born a genius, one becomes a genius.

Children must be taught how to think, not what to think.
Margaret Mead

Marie Curie
Be less curious about people and more curious about ideas.

Invite people into your life that don't look or think like you.
Mellody Hobson

For me, becoming isn't about arriving somewhere or achieving a certain aim. I see it instead as forward motion, a means of evolving, a way to reach continuously toward a better self. The journey doesn't end.
Michelle Obama

Margaret Atwood
War is what happens when language fails.

Ordinarily, I go to the woods alone, with not a single friend, for they are all smilers and talkers and therefore unsuitable.

I don't really want to be witnessed talking to the catbirds or hugging the old black oak tree. I have my way of praying, as you no doubt have yours.

Besides, when I am alone I can become invisible. I can sit on the top of a dune as motionless as an uprise of weeds, until the foxes run by unconcerned. I can hear the almost unhearable sound of the roses singing.

If you have ever gone to the woods with me, I must love you very much.
Mary Oliver

You can have it all. Just not all at once.
Oprah Winfrey

Each person must live their life as a model for others.
Rosa Parks

Fight for the things that you care about, but do it in a way
that will lead others to join you.
Ruth Bader Ginsburg

Beauty

Females are the most beautiful, gorgeous creatures in the whole world. And I think that we are gorgeous no matter what size we are.
Alicia Keys

Beauty lies not in a flawless complexion but in the stories that are told by each transitioning line on a woman's face.
Alyscia Cunningham

I say if I'm beautiful. I say if I'm strong. You will not determine my story—I will.
Amy Schumer

A woman whose smile is open and whose expression is glad has a kind of beauty no matter what she wears.
Anne Roiphe

I believe that happy girls are the prettiest girls.
Audrey Hepburn

The beauty of a woman is not in a facial mode, but the true beauty in a woman is reflected in her soul. It is the caring that she lovingly gives, the passion that she shows. The beauty of a woman grows with the passing years.
Audrey Hepburn

When you are balanced, and when you listen and attend to the needs of your body, mind, and spirit, your natural beauty comes out.
Christy Turlington

Beauty begins the moment you decide to be yourself.
Coco Chanel

You can be gorgeous at thirty, charming at forty, and irresistible for the rest of your life.
Coco Chanel

No matter how plain a woman may be, if truth and honesty are written across her face, she will be beautiful.
Eleanor Roosevelt

People are like stained-glass windows. They sparkle and shine when the sun is out, but when the darkness sets in, their true beauty is revealed only if there is a light from within.
Elisabeth Kubler-Ross

To me, beauty is about being comfortable in your own skin. It's about knowing and accepting who you are.
Ellen Degeneres

Beauty is not caused. It is.
Emily Dickinson

You don't have to be pretty. You don't owe prettiness to anyone. Not to your boyfriend/spouse/partner, not to your coworkers, especially not to random men on the street. You don't owe it to your mother, you don't owe it to your children, you don't owe it to civilization in general. Prettiness is not a rent you pay for occupying a space marked 'female'.
Erin McKean

Beauty shouldn't be about changing yourself to achieve an ideal or be more socially acceptable. Real beauty, the interesting, truly pleasing kind, is about honoring the beauty within you and without you. It's about knowing that someone else's definition of pretty has no hold over you.
Golda Poretsky

Outer beauty turns the head, but inner beauty turns the heart.
Helen J. Russell

Beauty is about enhancing what you have. Let yourself shine through.
Janelle Monae

What's the whole point of being pretty on the outside when you're so ugly on the inside?
Jess C. Scott

To tell the truth is to become beautiful, to begin to love yourself, value yourself. And that's political, in its most profound way.
June Jordan

Outer beauty attracts, but inner beauty captivates.
Kate Angell

There is no definition of beauty, but when you can see someone's spirit coming through, something unexplainable, that's beautiful to me.
Liv Tyler

I know people who've had a nose job, and they've walked out feeling like a million dollars, and their confidence is tenfold. Good on them! Natural beauty comes in all different shapes and sizes, but if you think surgery would right something you have a problem with, then why shouldn't you do it?
Louise Nurding

We too often bind ourselves by authorities rather than by the truth.
Lucretia Mott

I always thought that people told you that you're beautiful– that this was a title that was bestowed upon you … I think that it's time to take this power into our own hands and to say, 'You know what? I'm beautiful. I just am. And that's my light. I'm just a beautiful woman.
Margaret Cho

There is no cosmetic for beauty like happiness.
Maria Mitchell

We delight in the beauty of the butterfly, but rarely admit the changes it has gone through to achieve that beauty.
Maya Angelou

In the end, you will not see the physical beauty in others that caught your eye but the fire that burned within them.
Shannon L. Alder

Beauty is when you can appreciate yourself. When you love yourself, that's when you're most beautiful.
Zoë Kravitz

Time

One doesn't recognize the really important moments in one's life until it's too late.
Agatha Christie

Forever is composed of nows.
Emily Dickinson

Georgia O'Keeffe
Nobody sees a flower - really - it is so small it takes time - we haven't time - and to see takes time, like to have a friend takes time.

If you take a flower in your hand and really look at it, it's your world for a moment.
Georgia O'Keeffe

Margaret Atwood
Time is not a thing that passes ... it's a sea on which you float.

Peace is when time doesn't matter as it passes by.
Maria Schell

Please leave a review on Amazon:

Check out some of the books in the series:

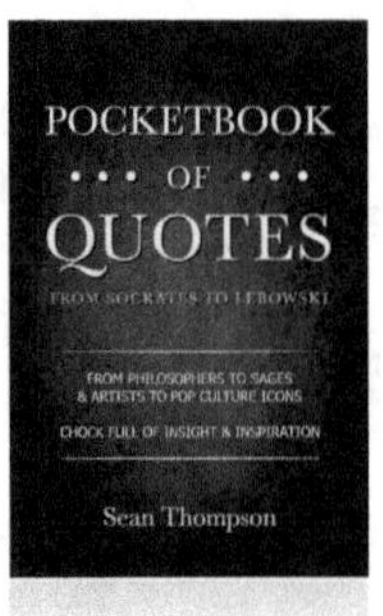

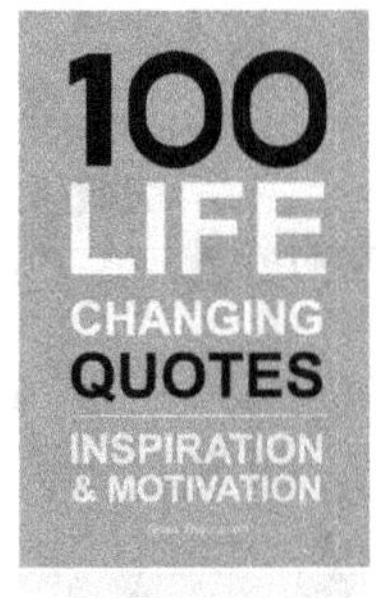

Check out the Facebook page:

* 9 7 9 8 3 3 9 4 1 5 0 3 9 *